The Goal Discussion Guide

The Goal Discussion Guide

Craig Paxson

New Salem Publishing - Nashville

'The Goal' Discussion Guide by Craig Paxson

Published by New Salem Publishing, Nashville, TN

First edition October 2019

ISBN 978-0-9863966-4-9 (paperback)

ISBN 978-0-9863966-3-2 (ebook)

Contents

Introduction

Early in 2015, I volunteered to lead a reading discussion group at work. The book I chose to read was *The Goal* by Eliyahu Goldratt. I scoured the Internet for a reading and discussion guide appropriate for a weekly group session and could not discover any. I found plenty of synopses and some college syllabi, but not any discussion guides. So, I decided to create one. This book is the discussion guide I created.

Because *The Goal* uses the Socratic Method: "ask – tell – ask," I decided to create the readings using that same method. Each week's reading begins with Alex asking a question of Jonah, then Jonah giving a response, Alex learning from that answer, and then we move on to the next question posed by Alex.

The discussion guide is broken into 7 weeks of reading. Each week's reading contains questions to be answered by the participants. Some weeks include exercises (for instance, the dice game played on the hike) that are designed to further illustrate the concepts discussed in the book. It will be helpful if the leader can customize the discussion questions and exercises for their particular organization.

Leader's Guide

How to Lead a Discussion of *The Goal*

Written as a novel, *The Goal* is transforming management thinking throughout the world. Alex Rogo is a harried plant manager working ever more desperately to try to improve performance. His factory is rapidly heading for disaster. So is his marriage. He has 90 days to save his plant – or corporate headquarters will close it, causing hundreds of job losses. It takes a chance meeting with Jonah, a professor from his student days, to help him break out of conventional ways of thinking and to see what needs to be done. The story of Alex's fight to save his plant is more than compelling reading. It contains a serious message for all managers in industry and explains the ideas that underlie the Theory of Constraints (TOC), developed by Eli Goldratt.

This is a seven-week discussion of *The Goal*. Each week you will read a selected set of chapters. The Goal is written using the Socratic Method: "ask - tell - ask." The chapters are selected based on the question that Jonah poses to Alex, what Alex learns and Alex's next questions. As you read each section, think about the following questions:

1. What is the current situation? What did Alex learn?
2. What questions does Alex currently have?
3. What hints does Jonah give Alex?
4. What answers will Alex discover?
5. How does this apply to my organization?

As discussion facilitator, you will ask questions designed to review the previous week's reading and may present exercises to enhance learning. You may download copies of the participant's discussion guide and a PowerPoint slide deck at www.craigpaxson.com/book/the-goal-discussion-guide.

For tips on running a book discussion group check out LitLovers at https://www.litlovers.com/run-a-book-club/lead-a-book-club-discussion.

Suggested Meeting Agenda

1. Review the previous reading. Ask the group to discuss questions 1 and 2 above
2. Review the reading specific questions and any related exercises
3. Review questions 3 and 4 above
4. Review question 5

Reading Schedule

Week 1: Introduction – Chapter 4

Week 2: Chapters 5 – 8

Week 3: Chapters 9 – 11

Week 4: Chapters 12 – 19

Week 5: Chapters 20 – 25

Week 6: Chapters 26 – 31

Week 7: Chapters 32 – 40

Characters

Alex Rogo: Plant manager

Jonah: Alex's college professor

Bill Peach: Division vice president

Lou: Plant controller

Stacey Potazenick: Inventory manager

Bob Donovan: Production manager

Ralph Nakamura: Data processing manager

Fran: Alex's secretary

Hilton Smyth: Division productivity manager and Alex's rival

Johnny Johns: Division vice president of sales

Herbie: Boy Scout who comes to symbolize the bottleneck in the plant

Introduction – Chapter 4

Key Events

- Bill Peach comes to Alex's plant demanding to know about order #41427 which is seven weeks overdue. The order must be shipped that day
- A machine needed for that order is down
- The plan works extra hours and ships the order
- The division must improve or be sold
- Alex remembers Jonah, his old professor, who understands Alex's dilemma
- Jonah's final question: What is Alex's company's goal?

Discussion

1. Why does Alex think the robots are so successful when he first talks to Jonah?

   - because their localized cost per part had gone down

2. How does Jonah indicate that the robots were not successful?

   - sales had not increased, labor had not decreased, and inventory had gone up

3. How does Jonah define productivity?

   - the act of bringing an organization closer to its goal. Every action that brings an organization closer to its goal is productive. Every action that does not bring an organization closer to its goal is not productive.

Next Meeting: Chapters 5 - 8

Chapters 5 – 8

Key Events

- Alex calls Jonah, who reveals three operational measurements:
    - Throughput is the rate at which the system generates money through sales.
    - Inventory is all the money that the system has invested in purchasing things that it intends to sell.
    - Operating expense is all the money the system spends in order to turn inventory into throughput.

Discussion

1. What is the goal?

   - Make money

2. What does your process manufacture?

3. What three common financial measures express the goal "to make money"?

   - Net Profit, Return on Investment and Cash Flow

4. Express the goal in terms of those financial measures

   - Increase net profit while simultaneously increasing both ROI and cash flow

5. What three measures are useful at the operational level to express the goal?

   - Throughput, Inventory and Operating Expense

6. Define throughput, inventory, and operating expense.

   - Throughput - the rate at which the system generates money through sales

     - Inventory - all the money the system has invested in purchasing things that it intends to sell

   - Operating Expense - all the money the system spends in order to turn inventory into throughput

7. Jonah claims the common financial measures are related to the operational measures. How?

- Net Profit = Throughput minus Operating Expense

- ROI = (Throughput minus Operating Expense) ÷ Inventory

- Cash Flow = Throughput –– Operating Expense ± ΔInventory

8. Define the measurements in your process' terms

- Throughput

- Inventory

- Operating Expense

9. What questions does Jonah leave Alex with? What do you think Alex will discover?

- Local Optimums

- Operational Rules

Next Meeting: Chapters 9 - 11

Chapters 9 – 11

Key Events

- The robots increased operating expenses without reducing labor
- Since inventory stayed the same, profit of the plant must have decreased
- Jonah states "A plant in which everyone is working all the time is very inefficient."
- Jonah asks Alex to consider "dependent events" and "statistical fluctuations."

Discussion – Definitions Quiz Cards

1. Express the "goal" in terms of throughput, inventory, and operating expense.

- Increase throughput while simultaneously decreasing inventory and cash flow

2. What is the result of high efficiencies on a non-constraint machine?

   - Excess inventory

3. Do high efficiencies necessarily imply higher profit?

   - No – high efficiencies lead to increased inventory unless that inventory is turned into throughput

4. Why is it important that throughput is defined in terms of sales rather than production?

- We don't get paid for finished goods

5. What causes a balanced plant to fail?

- Inventory and the carrying cost of inventory go up because of statistical fluctuations and dependent events

6. What are the types of operating expenses?

- Variable and Fixed, or

- Controllable and Uncontrollable

7. What is the equation for Productivity?

- Productivity = Throughput ÷ Operating Expense

8. What questions does Jonah leave Alex with? What do you think Alex will discover?

Next Meeting: Chapters 12 – 19

Definitions

Productivity - any action that moves the organization closer to the goal

The goal in financial measures - Increase net profit while simultaneously increasing both ROI and cash flow

Throughput - the rate at which the system generates money through sales

Inventory - all the money the system has invested in purchasing things which it intends to sell

Operating Expense - all the money the system spends in order to turn inventory into throughput

The Goal in operational measures - Increase throughput while simultaneously decreasing inventory and cash flow

Financial Measure Equations

Net Profit = Throughput – Operating Expense

ROI = (Throughput – Operating Expense) ÷ Inventory

Cash Flow = Throughput – Operating Expense ± ΔInventory

Productivity = Throughput ÷ Operating Expense

Chapters 12 – 19

Key Events

- On a hike with his son, Alex notices both statistical fluctuations and dependent events.
- Alex plays a dice game with the boys, further illustrating the problems that arise in his plant.
- Alex decides to let the slowest kid lead and the troop reaches their destination on time.
- Jonah tells Alex about the Theory of Constraints: "A bottleneck is any resource whose capacity is equal to or less than the demand placed upon it. A non-bottleneck is any resource whose capacity is greater than the demand placed on it."

Play the Dice Game (Appendix 2)

Discussion

1. Why does the spread of the line of Boy Scouts discussed on page 100 always become longer as time goes on?

   - The leaders are going faster than Herbie

2. What characteristics of the hiking troop relate to the production characteristics of throughput, inventory, and operating expense?

   - Throughput – the distance covered by the last scout in the troop

   - Inventory – the total length of the line

   - Operating Expense – energy expended by the troop

3. Using the hiking analogy on page 113, what happens in a plant if the fastest operations are put at the beginning of the production process, the slowest operations are put at the end, and all workers produce at high efficiency?

   - Inventory goes up

4. What is Herbie in terms of TOC?

   - The bottleneck or constraint

5. In terms of TOC, what has been done when Herbie goes to the front of the line?

   - Exploiting the constraint, letting the constraint dictate throughput

6. In terms of TOC, what was done when items are removed from Herbie's pack?

   - Elevating the constraint – making it go faster

7. Why was Pete so happy even though the order was not delivered on time?

   - Pete produced the 100 parts needed even though the total throughput was lower

8. Define a bottleneck

   - Any resource where capacity is less than demand

9. Why does Jonah say, "balance flow, not capacities"?

   - Each resource should only produce as much as the constraint

Next Meeting: Chapters 20 - 25

Chapters 20 – 25

Key Events

- The team prioritized the bottlenecks to work on the most overdue orders and devise a procedure to inform workers about overdue parts.
- The system works but new bottlenecks emerge
- Jonah visits the plant and the team discovers a new way to manage the flow of product through the plant.

Discussion

1. Why does Jonah say a plant should have bottlenecks?

   - Every production line has a bottleneck. It is impossible not to have one, so we should strive to utilize the bottleneck to meet operational goals

2. What does lost time at a bottleneck cost?

   - The throughput (revenue) or profit that could have been generated

3. What two things can be done to optimize a bottleneck?

   - Work only on things that contribute to throughput

   - Ensure there are always materials for the bottleneck to work on

4. What is the effect of the "efficient" operation of non-bottleneck machines?

   - Excess inventory

5. What determines the level of utilization of a non-bottleneck machine?

   - The level of utilization of a non-bottleneck is not determined by its own potential, but by some other constraint in the system

6. What are the combinations of production flow through a bottleneck and non-bottleneck?

   N -> B – non-bottleneck feeding bottleneck

   B -> N – bottleneck feeding non-bottleneck

B and N -> Assembly – bottleneck and non-bottleneck feeding assembly

B -> market and N -> market

7. What is the difference between activating a resource and utilizing a resource?

- Activating a resource is using it whether or not there is any benefit from its output

- utilizing a **resource** is using it in a way that moves the system toward the goal

8. Which resources in the system should we seek to optimize? Which should we not?

   - Optimize only the bottlenecks – constrain every other resource to the throughput of the bottleneck

9. What does Jonah suggest is the actual constraint in the system?

   - Policy – he says, "You created this monster by the decisions you made"

   10. What do you think is the solution Jonah is proposing?

Next Meeting: Chapters 26 - 31

Chapters 26 – 31

Key Events

- Alex can use the new production system to schedule when raw materials need to be released to production.
- Jonah tells Alex to cut batches in half.
- The same irate customer visits the plant to congratulate the team on shipping a rush order.

Discussion

1. What is the function of the drum and rope if used on a hike?

   - To keep everyone walking at the same pace, and keep everyone from getting spread out

2. What is the drum for the production facility?

   - The pace of the bottleneck

3. What is the rope for the production facility?

   - The total amount of work in process inventory

4. Why is a rope needed for assembly operations?

   - To ensure the correct amount of WIP and ensure bottlenecks do not run out of work

5. What is the next logical step after establishing the drum and rope for the production process?

   - Cut batch sizes – cutting WIP improves throughput (see Little's Law, Appendix 4)

6. What does cutting batch sizes in half for non-bottleneck operations accomplish?

   - It eases cash flow because less cash is tied in inventory

   - It improves throughput

7. How can the time the material spends in the plant be classified into four types?

Setup – time spent waiting for a resource while the resource is being prepared

Process – time spent while the resource is being worked on

Queue – waiting for a resource while that resource is busy on something else

Wait – for another part

8. What is time saved on a non-bottleneck machine?

- A mirage

This is a good time to bring up the concept of Little's Law. See the Appendix on Little's Law.

Play the Dot Game (Appendix 3) to illustrate the effect work-in-process inventory has on throughput, cycle time and cost.

Next Meeting: Chapters 32 - 40

Chapters 32 – 40

Key Events

- Alex promotes his team to run the plant
- The team formulates the five-step Process of Ongoing Improvement:
  Step 1: Identify the system's bottlenecks

  Step 2: Decide how to exploit those bottlenecks

  Step 3: Subordinate every other decision to 'step two decisions'

  Step 4: Elevate the system's bottlenecks

  Step 5: If, in a previous step, a bottleneck has been broken, go back to the beginning (Step 1).

- Alex finds a way to improve sales even more

Discussion

1. What are the 5 Focusing Steps?

    1. Identify the system constraint

    2. Exploit the constraint

    3. Subordinate everything to the constraint

    4. Elevate the constraint

    5. If a constraint has been broken, go back to Step 1, but do not allow inertia to cause a constraint

2. What is the Process of Change?

    1. What to Change

    2. What to Change To

    3. How to Cause the Change

3. Alex and his team have moved from the <u>Cost</u> world to the <u>Throughput</u> world.

4. In each world, what is the relative importance of Inventory (I), Operating Expense (OE) and Throughput (T) and why?

<u>Cost World</u>	<u>Throughput World</u>
1. Operating Expense	1. Throughput
2. Throughput	2. Inventory
3. Inventory	3. Operating Expense

5. What are your most important learnings?

Key Lessons

- Conventional management accounting metrics are wrong
- The three operational measurements:
    - Throughput: the rate at which the system generates money through sales net of variable costs. This corresponds to the value-added by the system.
    - Inventory: "all the money that system has invested in purchasing things which it intends to sell" This was later expanded to include all investment such as plant, property, equipment, etc.
    - Operating Expense: "all the money the system spends in order to turn inventory into throughput" These fixed costs like rent and salaries are incurred whether or not throughput increases or decreases.
- The slowest operation determines the maximum rate of the entire system (the bottleneck or constraint).
- The Process of Ongoing Improvement:
    1. Identify the system's constraint(s)
    2. Decide how to exploit the system's constraint(s)
    3. Subordinate everything else to exploit the constraint(s)
    4. Elevate the system's constraint(s)
    5. If in the previous steps, a constraint has been broken, go back to step 1, but do not allow inertia to cause a system constraint.

Appendix 1: Week 1 Quiz Cards

What is the definition of Productivity?	Express The Goal in operational measures
Express The Goal in financial measures	What is the equation for Net Profit in operational terms?
What is the definition of Throughput?	What is the equation for ROI in operational terms?
What is the definition of Inventory?	What is the equation for Cash Flow in operational terms?
What is the definition of Operating Expense?	

Appendix 2: The Dice Game

Adapted from the game played on the hike in Chapter 12

Purpose:

The dice game will demonstrate how variability and dependent events impact throughput.

Materials Required:

1 six-sided die

4 - 6 cups or bowls representing stages in the production process

Matches, pennies, poker chips or other items to move from bowl to bowl (minimum of 40).

Setup:

1. Set up a production line of 5 - 6 cups or bowls.

2. Place the tokens into the first bowl.

Game Play:

1. Worker 1 will roll the die and move the resulting number of tokens to the second cup in the line.

2. Worker 2 will roll the die and move the resulting number of tokens to the next cup in the process.

3. Repeat the procedure for the remaining workers. The last worker moves the tokens to "finished goods."

4. Each worker rolling the die and moving tokens counts as "1 day." You will play the game for 10 days.

5. Each student will record their roll and the number of tokens they moved during each turn.

Statistically, a single die can only roll six values, one each of 1, 2, 3, 4, 5 and 6. The average value for one roll is 3.5 (1+2+3+4+5+6=21 ÷ 6=3.5).

With 10 days of production, on average we would expect to move 3.5 tokens per day for a total of 35 tokens produced.

Discussion Questions:

1. How many tokens did the line produce? Versus what was expected?

2. How many tokens did each station produce versus what was expected?

3. What does this teach us about how variability and dependent events impact throughput?

Appendix 3: The Dot Game

Adapted from the Lean Manufacturing Cup Game

Purpose

The Dot game simulates a simple manufacturing system and demonstrates how work in process (WIP) inventory affects throughput, cycle time and cost.

Materials Required

2.5″ x 2.5″ Post-It Notes

4 colors of ¾ inch round stickers

Pen and Paper or Flipboard

Game Play:

The game requires between 4 and 6 players. Larger groups can have multiple "lines" or observers.

The "line" will manufacture a Post-It that looks like the one below. Make an example product and post it for the team to see.

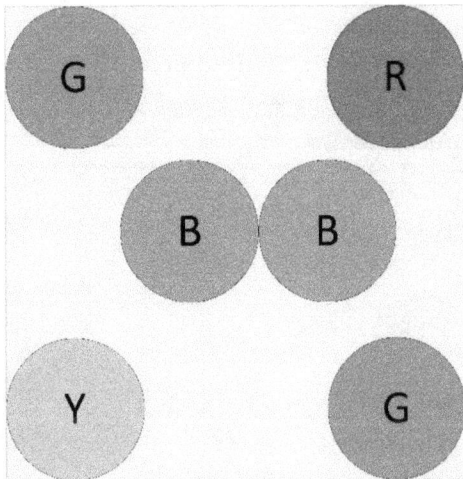

The

The line is broken into between 4 and 6 stations. You can adjust the number of stations based on the number of players.

Station 1 - Raw Materials. This player will tear off the requisite number of Post-Its and pass to the next station.

Station 2 - Red. This player will put on the one red dot.

Station 3- Blue. This player will put on the two blue dots.

Station 4 - Green. This player will put on the two green dots.

Station 5 - Yellow. This player will put on the one yellow dot.

Station 6 - Inspection. This player will inspect the Post-It and make sure it meets the standard.

The game is played in multiple rounds. Each round will be timed for 4 minutes.

Round 1 - Batches of 6. Each player will complete a batch of 6 Post Its prior to passing the entire batch of 6 to the next station. Record the number of Post-Its completed, the number remaining in WIP and the time for the first Post-It to be completed (Cycle Time).

Round 2 - Batches of 1. Each player will complete 1 Post-It and pass it to the next station. Record the number of Post-Its completed, the number remaining in WIP and the time for the first Post-It to be completed.

Scoring:

Throughput: The number of completed and correct Post-It notes.

WIP: The number of Post-It notes in process PLUS the number of dots affixed to Post-Its in process. For example, if a Post-It end between stations 3 and 4, it would have a WIP value of 4 (the Post-It plus 1 red dot plus 2 blue dots).

Discussion:

1. What effect did batch size have on Throughput?

2. Cycle Time

3. Cost?

Appendix 4: Little's Law

Little's Law states that inventory (I) is equal to cycle time (CT) multiplied by throughput (T). The equation looks like this:

Inventory (I) = Cycle Time (CT) x Throughput (T).

Alternatively, the law can represent Cycle Time:

CT = I ÷ T

Or Throughput:

T = I ÷ CT

The implications of Little's Law are that inventory management can control cycle time and throughput. We also know that as inventory rises, so does operating expense (because of carrying costs).

We also know from chapters 5 - 11 that:

Net Profit = Throughput – Operating Expense

ROI = (Throughput – Operating Expense) ÷ Inventory

Cash Flow = Throughput –– Operating Expense ± ΔInventory

Productivity = Throughput ÷ Operating Expense

Can you describe how cycle time fits into Jonah's operation terms and how it might affect productivity and net profit?

Participants Guide

Introduction

Early in 2015, I volunteered to lead a reading discussion group at work. The book I chose to read was *The Goal* by Eliyahu Goldratt. I scoured the Internet for a reading and discussion guide appropriate for a weekly group session and could not discover any. I found plenty of synopses and some college syllabi, but not any discussion guides. So I decided to create one. This book is the discussion guide I created.

Because *The Goal* uses the Socratic Method: "ask – tell – ask," I decided to create the readings using that same method. Each week's reading begins with Alex asking a question of Jonah, then Jonah giving a response, Alex learning from that answer, and then we move on to the next question posed by Alex.

The discussion guide is broken into 7 weeks of reading. Each week's reading includes questions to be answered by the participants. Some weeks include exercises (for instance, the dice game played on the hike) that are designed to further illustrate the concepts discussed in the book. It will be helpful if the leader can customize the discussion questions and exercises for their particular organization.

How to Read *The Goal*

Written as a novel, *The Goal* is transforming management thinking throughout the world. Alex Rogo is a harried plant manager working ever more desperately to try to improve performance. His factory is rapidly heading for disaster. So is his marriage. He has 90 days to save his plant – or corporate headquarters will close it, causing hundreds of job losses. It takes a chance meeting with Jonah, a professor from his student days, to help him break out of conventional ways of thinking to see what needs to be done. The story of Alex's fight to save his plant is more than compelling reading. It contains a serious message for all managers in industry and explains the ideas that underlie the Theory of Constraints (TOC), developed by Eli Goldratt.

This is a seven-week discussion of *The Goal*. Each week, you will read a selected set of chapters. The Goal is written using the Socratic Method: Ask - Tell - Ask. The chapters are selected based on the question that Jonah poses to Alex, what Alex learns and Alex's next questions. As you read each section, think about the following questions:

1. What is the current situation? What did Alex learn?
2. What questions does Alex currently have?
3. What hints does Jonah give Alex?
4. What do you think the answers Alex will discover are?
5. How does this apply to my organization?

Your discussion facilitator will ask questions that review the previous week's reading and may present exercises to enhance your learning.

Reading Schedule

Week 1 :Introduction – Chapter 4

Week 2: Chapters 5 – 8

Week 3: Chapters 9 – 11

Week 4: Chapters 12 – 19

Week 5: Chapters 20 – 25

Week 6: Chapters 26 – 31

Week 7: Chapters 32 – 40

Introduction – Chapter 4

1. When he first talks to Jonah, why does Alex think the robots are so successful?

2. How does Jonah indicate that the robots were not successful?

3. How does Jonah define productivity?

Next Meeting: Chapters 5 - 8

Chapters 5 – 8

1. What is the goal?

2. What does your process manufacture?

3. What three common financial measures express the goal "to make money"?

4. Express the "goal" in terms of those financial measures.

5. What three measures are useful at the operational level to express the goal?

6. Define throughput, inventory, and operating expense.

7. Jonah claims the common financial measures are related to the operational measures. How?

8. Define throughput, inventory and operating expense in your process' terms.

9. What questions does Jonah leave Alex with? What do you think Alex will discover?

Next Meeting: Chapters 9 - 11

Chapters 9 – 11

1. Express the "goal" in terms of throughput, inventory, and operating expense.

2. What is the result of high efficiencies occurring on a non-constraint machine?

3. Do high efficiencies necessarily imply higher profit?

4. Why is it important that throughput is defined in terms of sales rather than production?

5. What causes a balanced plant to fail?

6. What are the types of operational operating expenses?

7. What is the equation for productivity?

8. What questions does Jonah leave Alex with? What do you think Alex will discover?

Next Meeting: Chapters 12 - 19

Chapters 12 – 19

1. Why does the spread of the line of Boy Scouts discussed on page 100 always become longer as time goes on?

2. What characteristics of the hiking troop relate to the production characteristics of throughput, inventory, and operating expense?

3. Using the hiking analogy on page 113, what happens in a plant if the fastest operations are put at the beginning of the production process, the slowest operations are put at the end, and all workers produce at high efficiency?

4. What is Herbie in terms of TOC?

5. In terms of TOC, what has been done when Herbie goes to the front of the line?

6. In terms of TOC, what has been done when items are removed from Herbie's pack?

7. Why was Pete so happy even though the order was not delivered on time?

8. Define a bottleneck

9. Why does Jonah say, "balance flow, not capacities"?

The Dice Game

1. How many tokens did the line produce? Versus what was expected?

2. How many tokens did each station produce versus what was expected?

3. What does this teach us about how variability and dependent events impact throughput?

Next Meeting: Chapters 20 – 25

Chapters 20 – 25

1. Why does Jonah say a plant should have bottlenecks?

2. What does lost time at a bottleneck cost?

3. What two things can be done to optimize a bottleneck?

4. What is the effect of the "efficient" operation of non-bottleneck machines?

5. What determines the level of utilization of a non-bottleneck machine?

6. What are the combinations of production flow through a bottleneck and a non-bottleneck?

7. What is the difference between activating a resource and utilizing a resource?

8. Which resources in the system should we seek to optimize?

9. What does Jonah suggest is the actual constraint in the system?

10. What do you think is the solution Jonah is proposing?

Next Meeting: Chapters 26 – 31

Chapters 26 – 31

1. What are the functions of the drum and rope if used on a hike?

2. What is the drum for the production facility?

3. What is the rope for the production facility?

4. Why is a rope needed for assembly operations?

5. What is the next logical step after establishing the drum and rope for the production process?

6. What does cutting batch sizes in half for non-bottleneck operations accomplish?

7. How can the time the material spends in the plant be classified into four types?

8. What is time saved on a non-bottleneck machine?

The Dot Game

1. What effect did batch size have on Throughput?

2. Cycle Time

3. Cost?

Next Meeting: Chapters 32 – 40

Chapters 32 – 40

1. What are the 5 Focusing Steps?

2. What is the Process of Change?

3. Alex and his team have moved from the _____ world to the _____ world.

4. In each world, what is the relative importance of Inventory (I), Operating Expense (OE) and Throughput (T) and why?

_____ World   _____ World

1.   1.

2.   2.

3.   3.

5. What are your most important learnings?

About Eli Goldratt

Eli Goldratt is an educator, author, scientist, philosopher, and business leader. But he is, first and foremost, a thinker who provokes others to think. Often characterized as unconventional, stimulating, and "a slayer of sacred cows," Dr. Goldratt exhorts his audience to examine and reassess their business practices with a fresh, new vision.

He obtained his Bachelor of Science degree from Tel Aviv University and his Master of Science, and Doctor of Philosophy degrees from Bar-Ilan University. In addition to his pioneering work in business management and education, he holds patents in a number of areas ranging from medical devices to drip irrigation to temperature sensors.

Author Bio

Craig Paxson is a co-author of the best-selling business book *Unstuck: 10 Proven Strategies for Breaking Through the Barriers to Small Business Growth*. Craig is also the creator of the "Infinite Ideas" method of brainstorming and the "Process Innovation Framework," a simple yet powerful methodology for business process improvement.

For more information about Craig, his frameworks or books, please visit www.craigpaxson.com.

Further Reading

<u>Theory of Constraints</u>

It's Not Luck by Eli Goldratt

Applying TOC to sales and marketing

Critical Chain by Eli Goldratt

Applying TOC to project management

What is this thing called Theory of Constraints? by Eli Goldratt

Further explanation of the Five Focusing Steps, the Process of Change and implementing TOC

Breaking the Constraints to World-Class Performance by H. William Dettmer

Very in-depth discussion of the Theory of Constraints

<u>Lean</u>

Gemba Kaizen by Masaaki Imai

Applying the principles of lean production and continuous improvement

Office Kaizen by William Lareau

Applying the principles of lean production and continuous improvement to office and administrative functions